TERRY DURACK

Noodles

TERRY DURACK

Noodles

Photography by Philip Wilkins

WEIDENFELD & NICOLSON

Terry Durack

Terry Durack is Australia's most widely read and respected restaurant critic, food writer and noodle lover. As well as writing columns for the *Sydney Morning Herald* and *Australian Gourmet Traveller*, his articles appear regularly in the USA, Canada and Japan. He has written four books on food, including the highly acclaimed *Yum*, an autobiography with recipes. Much of his time is spent in Asia, commenting on food trends, judging food competitions and devouring noodles.

Contents

No food is really enjoyed
unless it is keenly anticipated,
discussed, eaten, and then
commented upon.

LIN YUTANG

Introduction

The world is waking up to noodles. If there is a more complete, more satisfying, more rewarding way to eat, then we haven't found it yet.

Noodles can be breakfast, lunch, dinner or a snack. They have been lusted after by emperors and beggars. They are healthy and nutritious. And they are great fun to cook, eat and serve among friends and family.

Here are twelve classic noodle dishes from Japan, Korea, China, Vietnam, Malaysia and Thailand, using ten different types of noodles. They are not just fast-fix, hotchpotch stir-fries, but truly great dishes that have form, structure, harmony, balance and history, not to mention certain amounts of chilli. Welcome to fine dining in its most slippery form.

Terry Durack

PAD THAI
Stir-fried noodles

SERVES 4

150 g/5 oz thin dried rice
   stick noodles*
1½ tablespoons tamarind pulp
1½ tablespoons palm sugar or
   brown sugar
3 tablespoons vegetable oil
3 garlic cloves, finely chopped
3 tablespoons dried shrimp,
   chopped
1 tablespoon salted radish,
   chopped
1 teaspoon dried chilli flakes
2 tablespoons fish sauce
150 g/5 oz beansprouts, rinsed
2 eggs, lightly beaten
2 tablespoons cubed firm tofu
   (beancurd)
20 garlic chives, cut into 5 cm/
   2 inch lengths
4 tablespoons roasted peanuts,
   lightly crushed
2–3 coriander sprigs

* known as sen lek in Thailand,
   banh pho in Vietnam

Soak the noodles in a saucepan of hot water for about 10 minutes, then bring to the boil and cook for about 2 minutes or until the noodles are tender. Strain, rinse in cold water, drain and set aside.

Combine the tamarind, sugar and 3 tablespoons boiling water in a bowl and stir until the sugar dissolves. Leave to stand for about 10 minutes, then strain off the liquid and set aside.

Heat a wok, then add 2 tablespoons of the oil. When hot, add the garlic, dried shrimp, radish and chilli and fry for 2 minutes, until the garlic just turns golden. Add the drained noodles and toss continually for 2–3 minutes. Add the tamarind liquid and fish sauce, and all but a handful of beansprouts.

Add the remaining tablespoon of oil to the wok. Move the noodles to one side of the wok and pour the eggs into the space created, scrambling them roughly. When the eggs start to set, cover with noodles and toss through. Add the tofu, garlic chives and the last handful of beansprouts. Tip out on to a warmed serving platter and scatter the crushed peanuts and coriander sprigs on top.

In Thailand, this is often accompanied by little dishes of more crushed peanuts, dried chillies and sugar to add at the table. Serve as part of a Thai meal with a hot and sour prawn soup (tom yam goong), Thai fishcakes with a sweet chilli dipping sauce, and a refreshing chilli and cucumber salad.

Laksa lemak
Curry noodle soup

SERVES 4

100 g/3½ oz dried rice vermicelli
4 cubes of fried beancurd puffs
2 tablespoons vegetable oil
laksa paste (page 37)
1.5 litres/2½ pints chicken stock
2 teaspoons palm sugar or
    brown sugar
1 teaspoon salt
500 ml/16 fl oz coconut milk
meat from half a cooked chicken,
    sliced
8 fish balls
8 uncooked prawns, peeled
200 g/7 oz fresh egg noodles
    (Hokkien noodles)
150 g/5 oz beansprouts
½ cucumber, peeled and cut
    into matchsticks
sprigs of fresh mint and
    coriander

Cook the rice vermicelli for 5–6 minutes in boiling water, then drain. Cut the beancurd puffs in half diagonally and set aside.

Heat a wok, then add the oil. When hot, add the laksa paste and fry for about 5 minutes, until fragrant. Add the stock, sugar and salt and bring to the boil. Reduce the heat and add the coconut milk, stirring constantly until it is hot. Add the chicken, fish balls and prawns and simmer gently for 2–3 minutes.

Put the drained rice vermicelli and fresh egg noodles into a large bowl, pour boiling water over them, then drain and rinse. Rinse the beansprouts with boiling water, then drain.

Divide the noodles and beancurd between four deep soup bowls. Using tongs, distribute the chicken, fish balls and prawns between the bowls, then top with hot soup. Arrange the cucumber and beansprouts on top, scatter with mint and coriander and serve at once.

Serve individual bowls of laksa lemak as a simple lunch, or as part of a Malaysian feast, along with chicken curry, roti bread, spinach fried with chilli and dried shrimp paste (blachan) and achar, or pickled vegetables.

HOKKIEN MEE
Fried noodles with pork and prawns

SERVES 4

400 g/14 oz fresh egg noodles
(Hokkien noodles)
2 dried red chillies, soaked in
water to cover for about
2 hours
200 g/7 oz squid, cleaned
200 g/7 oz uncooked prawns
in their shells
3 tablespoons peanut oil
250 ml/8 fl oz chicken stock
3 garlic cloves, crushed
200 g/7 oz Chinese roast pork
(char sieu) or leftover roast
pork, finely sliced
½ bunch of choi sum (flowering
cabbage), chopped
200 g/7 oz beansprouts, rinsed
in cold water
1 tablespoon dark soy sauce
2 tablespoons light soy sauce
2 spring onions, finely sliced

Put the noodles in a bowl, pour boiling water over them
and leave to stand for about 30 seconds, then drain and
rinse under cold water. Drain the chillies and chop.
Cut the squid into small squares and lightly score one
side in a criss-cross pattern. Shell the prawns, retaining
the heads and shells.

Heat 1 tablespoon of the oil in a wok and fry the prawn
heads and shells for 1 minute. Add the stock and simmer
for 5 minutes. Strain out the shells, return the stock to
the wok and add the prawns. Simmer gently until they
just turn white (about 1 minute). Remove the prawns
with a slotted spoon and set aside. Pour the stock into a
jug and set aside.

Heat the remaining oil in the wok. Add the garlic and
cook for 2–3 minutes, until the garlic turns golden,
then discard the garlic. Add the squid, pork and Chinese
cabbage and stir-fry over high heat for 2 minutes. Add
the prawns and beansprouts and stir-fry for 1 minute.
Add the noodles and stir-fry for 1–2 minutes, tossing
constantly, then add the stock, soy sauces and spring
onions and cook until everything is hot. Serve at once.

*Create a Singapore-style feast by starting with beef rib soup
(bah kut teh). Serve Hokkien mee along with deep-fried
chicken (enche kebin) and rojak, a refreshing fruit and
vegetable salad.*

Zaru soba
Chilled soba noodles with dipping sauce

SERVES 4

350 g/13 oz dried buckwheat
   noodles (soba)
500 ml/16 fl oz dashi (page 36)
4 tablespoons Japanese
   soy sauce
4 tablespoons mirin
½ teaspoon sugar
1 sheet dried nori seaweed
1 teaspoon wasabi powder,
   mixed to a paste with a
   little water
3 spring onions, finely sliced

Bring a large saucepan of water to the boil and add the noodles. When the water returns to the boil, add 250 ml/8 fl oz cold water. Repeat the process, then continue to boil until the noodles are just past al dente (firm, but cooked through). Drain the noodles and plunge them into cold water, washing them with your hands to remove all the starch. Drain and chill.

Put the dashi, soy sauce, mirin and sugar in a saucepan, bring to the boil, stirring frequently, then cool and chill in the refrigerator.

When ready to serve, divide the noodles between four shallow bowls or slatted bamboo boxes. Lightly toast the nori over a gas flame or under a hot grill until crisp, then cut with scissors into long, thin strips and arrange over the noodles.

Divide the chilled sauce between four small serving bowls. Each diner picks up some noodles with chopsticks and dips them into the sauce, adding wasabi and spring onions to taste.

Serve on a warm summer's day as part of a simple Japanese meal, along with a dish of vinegared crab, clams in butter sauce, grilled aubergine and salted mackerel. Finish with a platter of carved fresh fruit.

WON TON NOODLE SOUP
Dumpling soup with noodles

SERVES 4

150 g/5 oz uncooked prawns,
    finely chopped
150 g/5 oz minced pork
2 tablespoons finely chopped
    pork or bacon fat
4 dried shiitake mushrooms,
    soaked in warm water for
    1–2 hours, then drained
    and finely chopped
4 water chestnuts,
    finely chopped
2 spring onions, finely chopped
1 small egg white
salt and pepper
200 g/7 oz fresh thin egg
    noodles
1 packet fresh won ton wrappers
1 heaped teaspoon cornflour
    blended with 1 tablespoon
    cold water
1.5 litres/2½ pints good
    chicken stock
2 slices of fresh ginger
100 g/4 oz choi sum (flowering
    cabbage), roughly sliced
2 spring onions, sliced

To make the dumplings, put the prawns, pork, pork fat, mushrooms, water chestnuts, chopped spring onions, egg white, salt and pepper in a bowl and mix with your hands until totally amalgamated. Chill in the refrigerator for 1–2 hours.

Put the noodles in a bowl, pour boiling water over them and leave for 1–2 minutes or until they soften. Rinse under cold water, drain and set aside.

Lay a won ton wrapper on the work surface. Place up to a teaspoon of filling in the centre. Dip your finger into the cornflour paste and run it around the edges. Fold over to form a triangle, pressing the edges together. Now bring the two outer corners together to meet and overlap in the middle, and seal with a little paste. Allow four or five won tons per person.

Put the stock into a wide saucepan, add the ginger and bring to a gentle simmer. Blanch the Chinese cabbage in boiling water for 1 minute, then drain and add to the stock. Rinse the noodles in boiling water, drain, then divide between four warmed deep soup bowls.

Place the won tons in a saucepan of boiling water and simmer until they float to the surface. Drain and distribute between the bowls. Discard the ginger and pour the hot stock over the won tons. Sprinkle with sliced spring onions.

This is the perfect lunch in a bowl, but could also be made part of a shared Cantonese meal, by adding a plate of steamed Chinese sausage (lup cheong), and crisp pork and mushroom spring rolls. Finish with fresh lychees or sliced oranges.

HOR FUN WITH BEEF
Fried rice noodles with beef

SERVES 4

5 tablespoons peanut oil
200 g/7 oz lean beef,
    thinly sliced
1 tablespoon light soy sauce
1 teaspoon cornflour blended
    with 1 tablespoon cold water
600 g/1¼ lb fresh rice
    sheet noodles*
1 teaspoon sugar
2 tablespoons dark soy sauce
2 slices of fresh ginger, shredded
2 spring onions, finely chopped
a generous handful of
    beansprouts, rinsed

* known as hor fun or he fen in
    China, pho in Vietnam and
    kueh teow in Malaysia

Heat the oil in a wok. When hot, leave over the heat for 2 minutes, then leave to cool. (This 'cooked' oil is necessary for an authentic flavour.)

Mix 2 tablespoons of the oil with the beef, the light soy sauce and the cornflour mixture and leave to marinate for 30 minutes.

If the rice sheets are not pre-cut, cut them into 2 cm/¾ inch strips, like tagliatelle. Place in a bowl and pour boiling water over them to cover, gently shaking the strips apart with a pair of chopsticks. Immediately drain and rinse under cold running water and set aside.

Mix the sugar with the dark soy sauce and set aside.

Heat a wok, then add the remaining oil. When hot, add the ginger and cook for 1 minute. Add the beef mixture and stir-fry until it changes colour, about 1 minute. Add the beansprouts and stir-fry for 1 minute. Lift out and set aside.

Add the drained noodles to the wok, together with the sugar and soy sauce mixture, and stir well for 2 minutes. Return the beef to the wok and stir-fry until everything is hot, sprinkle the spring onions on top and serve at once.

A favourite lunch or supper dish, this also works as part of a Cantonese dinner. Serve with prawns steamed in their shells, and steamed Chinese vegetables with shiitake mushrooms. Finish with a traditional Cantonese sweet walnut soup.

Pho Ga
Chicken noodle soup

SERVES 4

1 whole chicken, preferably with
   head and feet
1 kg/2¼ lb chicken bones
2 onions, 1 quartered, 1 sliced
   paper-thin
1 teaspoon salt
5 cm/2 inch piece of fresh
   ginger, sliced
1 cinnamon stick
1 star anise
3 cardamom pods
2 teaspoons sugar
3 tablespoons fried shallots
3 tablespoons fish sauce
400 g/14 oz fresh rice
   sheet noodles
4 spring onions, finely sliced
8 sprigs of coriander

To serve
a generous handful
   of beansprouts
sprigs of mint
sprigs of holy basil (sweet
   Asian basil)
sprigs of coriander
1 fresh red chilli, finely chopped
1 lemon or lime, cut into wedges

Put the whole chicken and the bones into a large
saucepan with the quartered onion, the salt, ginger,
cinnamon, star anise, cardamom and 3 litres/2½ pints
water. Bring to the boil. Skim off any froth that rises
to the surface, then lower the heat and simmer for
1½ hours. Remove the chicken and set aside.

Add the sugar, 2 tablespoons of the fried shallots and
the fish sauce to the stock and cook for a further hour.
Strain the stock through a fine sieve.

Slice the chicken thigh and breast meat into fine slices.

If not pre-cut, cut the rice noodles into 1 cm/½ inch
strips, like tagliatelle. Place in a bowl and pour boiling
water over them to cover, gently shaking the strips apart
with a pair of chopsticks. Drain, then divide the noodles
between four deep soup bowls. Layer the chicken meat
neatly on top along with a few onion slices, and spoon
some hot soup into each bowl. Scatter the remaining
fried shallots and the coriander on top.

Serve with an accompanying platter of beansprouts,
fresh herbs, chopped chilli and lemon or lime wedges,
for each person to add according to their taste.

*In Vietnam, this is a self-sufficient breakfast in a bowl. You can
turn it into a satisfying lunch or dinner by adding a plate of
Vietnamese spring rolls with a sweet chilli dipping sauce.*

MEE KROB
Crisp fried noodles

SERVES 4

2 tablespoons palm sugar
   or brown sugar
2 tablespoons fish sauce*
2 tablespoons fresh lime or
   lemon juice
1 tablespoon rice vinegar
175 g/6 oz dried rice vermicelli
vegetable oil for deep-frying
2 garlic cloves, finely chopped
6 shallots, finely chopped
225 g/8 oz minced pork
   or chicken
200 g/7 oz uncooked prawns,
   finely chopped
125 g/4 oz firm tofu (beancurd),
   diced
2 fresh red chillies, sliced
2 eggs, lightly beaten
100 g/3½ oz beansprouts, rinsed
a generous handful of
   coriander leaves
3 spring onions (green parts),
   finely chopped

* known as nam pla in Thailand,
   nuoc mam in Vietnam

Put the sugar, fish sauce, lime juice and vinegar into a saucepan and bring to the boil, stirring constantly. Allow to bubble for 3–4 minutes, until the liquid reduces in volume by one-third and starts to turn dark and sticky. Keep warm.

Put the uncooked noodles in a large bowl and break into short lengths. Heat the oil in a wok until it begins to smoke, then add a handful of noodles at a time to the oil. Immediately they puff up, use a large slotted spoon to flip them over for 1 second, then, before they begin to turn brown, remove and drain on paper towels. Keep the noodles warm in a low oven.

Pour off all but 2 tablespoons of the oil and fry the garlic and shallots until they start to colour. Add the pork or chicken, prawns, beancurd and one of the chillies and stir-fry for about 3 minutes.

Add the eggs a little at a time, stirring constantly, until cooked. Add the vinegar liquid and beansprouts and toss well until steaming hot.

Arrange the crisp fried noodles on a large platter and spoon the mixture in the centre. Pile a few crisp noodles on top and scatter with coriander, spring onions and the remaining chilli. Serve immediately, as the noodles will soften after about 10 minutes.

Create a full-flavoured Thai dinner by serving alongside a green chicken curry, a platter of fresh raw vegetables with a chilli dip, and som tum, a refreshing green papaya salad. Finish with sticky rice and mango drizzled with coconut cream.

Nabeyaki udon
Udon noodles in broth with tempura

SERVES 2

1 chicken thigh, boned and cut
   into bite-sized pieces
2½ tablespoons Japanese
   soy sauce
4 teaspoons mirin
150 g/5 oz dried udon noodles
750 ml/1¼ pints dashi
   (page 36)
2 teaspoons sugar
pinch of salt
2 dried shiitake mushrooms,
   soaked in warm water for
   1–2 hours
½ Japanese fish cake
   (kamaboko), finely sliced
½ tablespoon dried wakame
   seaweed
vegetable oil for deep-frying
2 large uncooked prawns,
   peeled, tails left on
about 1 tablespoon plain flour
tempura batter (page 37)
1 large egg
2 spring onions, cut into 6 cm/
   2½ inch lengths

Put the chicken in a small bowl with 1 teaspoon of the soy sauce and 1 teaspoon of the mirin and leave to marinate for 30 minutes.

Bring a large saucepan of water to the boil and add the noodles. When the water returns to the boil, add 250 ml/8 fl oz cold water. Repeat the process three times, until the noodles are cooked and tender, about 10 minutes. Drain, rinse under cold water and set aside.

In a casserole or claypot, combine the dashi, sugar, salt and the remaining soy sauce and mirin, and bring to the boil. Add the mushrooms, fishcake slices and chicken and simmer gently for 15 minutes.

Meanwhile, soak the wakame in cold water for 10 minutes. Drain and set aside.

Heat the oil in a wok until it begins to smoke. Dredge the prawns in flour, dip each one into the tempura batter and drop into the hot oil. Deep-fry for about 2 minutes, until the batter is lightly golden and crisp.

Rinse the noodles in boiling water, then add to the soup and bring to the boil. Break the egg on top of the noodles, add the spring onions and cover the pot for about 1 minute, until the egg white is just cooked. Arrange the tempura prawns on top and bring to the table. Break the egg with chopsticks and stir through.

Traditionally, nabeyaki udon is served in individual bowls, with one egg per person, as a meal in a bowl. This version is for two to share in one large bowl. Turn it into a meal by starting with sushi or sashimi. Finish with green tea ice cream, fresh fruit and Japanese tea.

DAN DAN NOODLES
Chilled spicy noodles

SERVES 4

1 small piece of fresh ginger,
    sliced into matchsticks
1 teaspoon vegetable oil
3 teaspoons sugar
500 g/1 lb 2 oz fresh flat
    Chinese wheat noodles
3 teaspoons peanut oil
2 teaspoons sesame oil
a generous handful
    of beansprouts
1 tablespoon sesame seeds
3 tablespoons sesame paste,
    tahini or peanut butter
2–3 teaspoons Sichuan chilli oil
    (page 36)
2 tablespoons light soy sauce
1 tablespoon Chinese
    black vinegar or rice vinegar
½ teaspoon Sichuan pepper or
    black peppercorns, crushed
2 spring onions, finely chopped

Put the ginger in a small bowl with the vegetable oil and 1 teaspoon of the sugar and leave to marinate for 1 hour.

Put the noodles in a saucepan of boiling water and cook for 2–3 minutes, until tender. Rinse in cold water, drain and shake dry. Add 1 teaspoon each of the peanut oil and sesame oil, and toss to prevent the noodles from sticking.

Pour boiling water over the beansprouts, drain, rinse and shake dry.

Toast the sesame seeds in a dry pan until they just start to turn brown. Crush lightly.

Mix the remaining peanut oil and sesame oil with the sesame paste, chilli oil, 3 tablespoons water and the toasted sesame seeds. Add the soy sauce, vinegar, pepper and the remaining sugar. Pour the sauce over the cold noodles and top with beansprouts, marinated ginger and spring onions.

Serve as part of a Sichuan banquet with dry-fried shredded chilli beef, tea-smoked duck and Mandarin pancakes. Finish with sweet walnuts, fresh mandarins or lychees.

CHAP CHAE
Stir-fried noodles with beef and vegetables

SERVES 4–6

2 tablespoons wood ear
    fungus or 6 dried shiitake
    mushrooms, soaked in warm
    water for 2 hours
1 tablespoon sesame seeds
400 g/14 oz good quality beef,
    cut into thick matchsticks
4 garlic cloves, crushed
2 spring onions, thinly sliced
2 teaspoons sugar
5 tablespoons dark soy sauce
1 tablespoon sesame oil
250 g/9 oz cellophane (bean
    thread) noodles
5 tablespoons vegetable oil
2 eggs, lightly beaten
½ carrot, cut into matchsticks
1 onion, sliced lengthways
    into slivers
a generous handful of
    beansprouts, rinsed
½ head of Chinese leaves
    (Peking cabbage) or Savoy
    cabbage, shredded
½ cucumber, cut into
    matchsticks
salt

Drain the fungus or mushrooms and cut into fine strips.
Toast the sesame seeds in a dry pan until they just start
to turn golden.

Put the beef in a bowl with the sesame seeds, garlic,
spring onions, 1 teaspoon of the sugar, 2 tablespoons of
the soy sauce and 1 teaspoon of the sesame oil, and leave
to marinate for 1 hour.

Soak the noodles in hot water for about 15 minutes
or until soft. Rinse in cold water, drain and cut into
10 cm/4 inch lengths.

Heat a wok, then add 1 tablespoon of the vegetable oil,
swirling the wok to coat the entire surface. Pour in the
eggs and swirl around the wok to form a thin omelette.
When the omelette has just set, remove it from the wok.
Roll into a cylinder, cut into thin strips and set aside.

Add 2 tablespoons of the vegetable oil to the wok and
heat through. Add the carrot and onion and stir-fry until
they soften, then add the beansprouts and cabbage and
stir-fry for a further 2 minutes. Add the cucumber and
toss through, then tip out on to a plate and keep warm.

Heat the remaining 2 tablespoons of oil in the wok,
add the beef mixture and the fungus or mushroom
strips and stir-fry for 2 minutes. Add the noodles, the
remaining soy sauce, sesame oil, sugar and a pinch of
salt. Return the vegetables to the wok, heat through
and serve scattered with omelette strips.

*This is a simple family meal. When entertaining, begin
with Korean oxtail soup then serve chap chae, with preserved
cabbage (kim chee) and chicken cooked with ginseng.*

CHUNGKING NOODLES
Transparent noodles with pork

SERVES 2–4

200 g/7 oz minced pork
2 tablespoons light soy sauce
1 tablespoon sugar
1 teaspoon cornflour
1 teaspoon soybean and chilli
   paste, or chilli sauce
100 g/3½ oz bean thread
   noodles
3 tablespoons vegetable oil
1 small fresh red chilli
2 spring onions, finely chopped
125 ml/4 fl oz chicken stock
   or water
1 tablespoon dark soy sauce
2 spring onions, thinly sliced

Mix the minced pork with the light soy sauce, sugar, cornflour and soybean and chilli paste or sauce. Leave to marinate for about 30 minutes.

Soak the noodles in hot water for 10 minutes or until soft, then drain.

Heat a wok and add the oil. When hot, add the chilli and chopped spring onions, then the pork and its marinade, stirring well. When the meat starts to brown, add the drained noodles and stir well.

Add the chicken stock or water and dark soy sauce and continue to cook until the noodles absorb all the liquid. Turn out on to a warm serving platter and surround with sliced spring onions.

Serve as part of a Western Chinese meal, with hot and sour soup, sweet-and-sour spare ribs and braised aubergine.

The Basics

GLOSSARY OF INGREDIENTS

BEANCURD (TOFU)
Beancurd, made from soybeans, is sold in vacuum packs in many supermarkets; for stir-frying look for firm rather than 'silken' tofu. Asian food stores also sell beancurd 'puffs', cubes of deep-fried beancurd.

BONITO FLAKES
Dried shavings of a fish of the mackerel family, used in making dashi stock and for flavouring Japanese soups.

CANDLENUTS
Round nuts, similar to macadamias, used to thicken and add a sweet nutty flavour to Thai and Malaysian dishes.

CHINESE RICE WINE
A yellow wine made from glutinous rice, used in marinades, stir-fries and braised dishes.

CHINESE ROAST PORK
Chinese red roasted pork (*char sieu*), available from Asian food stores and some supermarkets.

FISH BALLS
Cooked balls of minced fish, used in soups and stir-fries. Found in the refrigerated section of Asian food stores.

FISH SAUCE
A pungent, salty sauce made from fermented fish, known as *nuoc mam* in Vietnam and *nam pla* in Thailand.

GALANGAL
Also known as laos and Siamese ginger, galangal has a medicinal taste and woody texture, and is an essential flavour in Thai cooking.

KAMABOKO
White Japanese fishcake pressed on to a thin flat board. Usually sold frozen in Asian food stores.

KONBU
Giant sea kelp, usually sold dried. Along with bonito, it forms the basis of Japanese dashi stock.

MIRIN

Sweet rice wine with low alcohol content, used in Japanese cooking.

NORI

Dark green sheets of dried seaweed, used to wrap rice in rolls, and to garnish savoury dishes.

PALM SUGAR

Sugar made from the sap of various palm trees, usually sold in blocks. Scrape with a knife or cut off small pieces and dissolve in hot water. If unavailable, substitute light soft brown sugar.

SALTED RADISH

A dried and salted root vegetable known as *hua pak gart kao* in Thailand. It may be labelled 'salted turnip'.

SESAME PASTE

A paste made from crushed sesame seeds. Substitute tahini or smooth peanut butter.

SICHUAN PEPPER

The seeds from the peppery ash tree, with a peppery, prickly flavour.

SICHUAN PRESERVED VEGETABLE

Mustard green roots preserved in salt and chilli and usually sold in cans.

SOYBEAN AND CHILLI PASTE

A pungent, thick chilli sauce, chunky with soybeans, sold in jars at Asian food stores.

TAMARIND

Sour-tasting tamarind pulp is extracted from the pods of tamarind trees and compressed into blocks. To make tamarind water, mix tamarind pulp with boiling water, let stand for 10 minutes, then strain and use the liquid. Lemon juice can be substituted, but it lacks depth.

WAKAME

Dark green dried seaweed which expands dramatically when soaked in water. Used to flavour soups.

WASABI

A green pungent root known as Japanese horseradish, it is grated to form a paste with the bite and kick of English mustard. Available in Asian supermarkets in tubes or powdered in tins.

WON TON WRAPPERS

Thin sheets of dough, about 10 cm/4 inches square, made from eggs and wheat flour. Even professionals use the ready-made sheets, available at Asian food stores.

WOOD EAR FUNGUS

Also known as cloud ear fungus, this is a black fungus which grows on decayed wood. It is sold dried and expands to many times its size when soaked. Trim off the hard stems before using.

SICHUAN CHILLI OIL
250 ml/8 fl oz peanut oil
3 tablespoons dried red chillies,
    crushed
1 teaspoon Sichuan peppercorns

Heat the oil in a wok until almost smoking, then turn off the heat. Add the chillies and peppercorns and leave to cool. Strain through a fine sieve or muslin into a screw-topped bottle and store in a cool, dark place.

DASHI
1 litre/1¾ pints cold water
8 cm/3 inch square piece
    of konbu (kelp)
25 g/1 oz dried bonito flakes

Put the water in a saucepan with the konbu and heat. Just before the water comes to the boil, remove the konbu and add the bonito flakes. Bring back to the boil, then immediately remove the pan from the heat. Leave for 30 seconds to 1 minute, then strain through muslin and leave to cool.

TEMPURA BATTER

1 egg yolk
250 ml/8 fl oz iced water
125 g/4 oz plain flour, sifted

Put the egg yolk in a bowl. Add the iced water and mix with chopsticks – do not beat. Add the flour all at once, and mix lightly; the mixture should still be rough and lumpy. Don't overmix, or the batter will be heavy.

LAKSA PASTE

1 onion, finely chopped
1 tablespoon grated
    fresh ginger
1 tablespoon grated
    fresh galangal
2 garlic cloves, chopped
2 stalks of lemongrass, white
    part only, sliced
6 dried red chillies, soaked
    for about 2 hours,
    then chopped
4 candlenuts or macadamia
    nuts, crushed
1 teaspoon ground coriander
1 teaspoon paprika
1 teaspoon ground cumin
6 laksa or Asian mint leaves
1 teaspoon turmeric
1 tablespoon Asian shrimp
    paste (blachan)

Put all the ingredients into a mortar and pound with a pestle for 10–15 minutes, until a thick, fragrant, amalgamated paste is formed. Alternatively, blend in a food processor, adding the ingredients gradually.

Classic Cooking

STARTERS
Lesley Waters A former chef and now a popular television cook, appearing regularly on *Ready Steady Cook* and *Can't Cook Won't Cook*. Author of several cookery books.

VEGETABLE SOUPS
Elisabeth Luard Cookery writer for the *Sunday Telegraph Magazine* and author of *European Peasant Food* and *European Festival Food*, which won a Glenfiddich Award.

GOURMET SALADS
Sonia Stevenson The first woman chef in the UK to be awarded a Michelin star, at the Horn of Plenty in Devon. Author of *The Magic of Saucery* and *Fresh Ways with Fish*.

FISH AND SHELLFISH
Gordon Ramsay Chef/proprietor of London's Aubergine restaurant, recently awarded its second Michelin star, and author of *A Passion for Flavour*.

CHICKEN, DUCK AND GAME
Nick Nairn Chef/patron of Braeval restaurant near Aberfoyle in Scotland, whose BBC-TV series *Wild Harvest* was last summer's most successful cookery series, accompanied by a book.

LIVERS, SWEETBREADS AND KIDNEYS
Simon Hopkinson Former chef/patron at London's Bibendum restaurant, columnist and author of *Roast Chicken and Other Stories* and *The Prawn Cocktail Years*.

VEGETARIAN
Rosamond Richardson Author of several vegetarian titles, including *The Great Green Cookbook* and *Food from Green Places*.

PASTA
Joy Davies One of the creators of *BBC Good Food Magazine*, she has been food editor of *She, Woman* and *Options* and written for the *Guardian*, *Daily Telegraph* and *Harpers & Queen*.

CHEESE DISHES
Rose Elliot The UK's most successful vegetarian cookery writer and author of many books, including *Not Just a Load of Old Lentils* and *The Classic Vegetarian Cookbook*.

POTATO DISHES
Patrick McDonald Former chef/patron of the acclaimed Epicurean restaurant in Cheltenham, and food consultant to Sir Rocco Forte Hotels.

BISTRO
Anne Willan Founder and director of La Varenne Cookery School in Burgundy and West Virginia. Author of many books and a specialist in French cuisine.

ITALIAN
Anna Del Conte Author of several books on Italian food, including *The Gastronomy of Italy*, *Secrets from an Italian Kitchen* and *The Classic Food of Northern Italy* (chosen as the 1996 Guild of Food Writers Book of the Year).

VIETNAMESE
Nicole Routhier One of the United States' most popular cookery writers, her books include *Cooking Under Wraps, Nicole Routhier's Fruit Cookbook* and the award-winning *The Foods of Vietnam.*

MALAYSIAN
Jill Dupleix One of Australia's best known cookery writers and broadcasters, with columns in the *Sydney Morning Herald* and *Elle.* Her books include *New Food* and *Allegro al dente.*

PEKING CUISINE
Helen Chen Author of *Chinese Home Cooking,* she learned to cook traditional Peking dishes from her mother, Joyce Chen, the *grande dame* of Chinese cooking in the United States.

STIR-FRIES
Kay Fairfax A writer and broadcaster whose books include *100 Great Stir-fries, Homemade* and *The Australian Christmas Book.*

NOODLES
Terry Durack Australia's most widely read restaurant critic and co-editor of the *Sydney Morning Herald Good Food Guide.* He is the author of *YUM,* a book of stories and recipes.

NORTH INDIAN CURRIES
Pat Chapman Founded the Curry Club in 1982. A regular broadcaster on television and radio, he is the author of 20 books, which have sold more than 1 million copies.

GRILLS AND BARBECUES
Brian Turner Chef/patron of Turner's in Knightsbridge and one of Britain's most popular food broadcasters; he appears frequently on *Ready Steady Cook, Food and Drink* and many other television programmes.

SUMMER AND WINTER CASSEROLES
Anton Edelmann Maître Chef des Cuisines at the Savoy Hotel, London. Author of six cookery books, he has also appeared on television.

TRADITIONAL PUDDINGS
Tessa Bramley Chef/patron of the acclaimed Old Vicarage restaurant in Ridgeway, Derbyshire and author of *The Instinctive Cook.*

DECORATED CAKES
Jane Asher Author of several cookery books and a novel. She has also appeared in her own television series, *Jane Asher's Christmas* (1995).

FAVOURITE CAKES
Mary Berry One of Britain's leading cookery writers, her numerous books include *Mary Berry's Ultimate Cake Book.* She has made many television and radio appearances.

ICE CREAMS AND SEMI FREDDI
Ann and Franco Taruschio Owners of the renowned Walnut Tree Inn near Abergavenny in Wales, soon to appear in a television series, *Franco and Friends: Food from the Walnut Tree.* They have written three books together.

Text © Terry Durack 1997

Terry Durack has asserted his right to be identified
as the author of this Work.

Photographs © Philip Wilkins 1997

First published in 1997 by
George Weidenfeld & Nicolson
The Orion Publishing Group
Orion House
5 Upper St Martin's Lane
London WC2H 9EA

British Library Cataloguing-in-Publication data
A catalogue record for this book is available from
the British Library

ISBN 0 297 82276 4

Designed by Lucy Holmes
Edited by Maggie Ramsay
Food styling by Louise Pickford
Typesetting by Tiger Typeset